Note to Parents and Teachers

If a child asked, "What's the Bible all about?" how would you answer? This could be more difficult than you think . . . "Uh, well the Bible is about . . . God, Jesus, sin, salvation . . . going to heaven . . . being good . . . doctrine." All these are important, yet none qualify as the Bible's "big picture."

Part of the problem is how we've come to view the Bible. We see sixty-six separate books instead of *one* story—*God's* Story. Because we've not been clear on this ourselves, we've not been able to make it clear to our children. As a result, kids raised in the church hear a lot of Bible stories. But rarely do they see how these fit together into one story. In other words, we teach Bible stories, but not the *Bible's Story.*

So what is the Bible all about? Simply this—God wants to live in friendship (relationship) with us both now and forever. We see this in Genesis where God walked in the garden with Adam and Eve and in Revelation: "Behold, the tabernacle of God is among men, and He will dwell among them" (Revelation 21:3).

The Big Picture of What God Has Always Wanted highlights God's desire to live with His people using a kid-friendly storyline. This overview of the Bible will help you and your child see what the Bible is really all about.

Chances are, what God has always wanted is what you want for your child, too. At the end of the story, your child may wonder: *Am I one of God's friends?* At this point, read the "What About You?" section on page 22. It sets you up to invite your child into a relationship with God using simple, accurate language.

The importance of simple, accurate language can't be stressed enough. I understand how in simplifying the gospel for kids, we tend to share a few truths and then urge children to "ask Jesus into your heart." This approach is well-intended, but it may confuse children. Nowhere does the Bible say "ask Jesus into your heart." Since children think concretely, they often picture a miniature Jesus coming into a valentine-shaped heart. This metaphor can make the gospel unclear.

But Jesus' invitation is clear. We receive eternal life by "believing in Him."* If children know what it means to trust a friend to keep a promise, then they can understand what it means to trust Jesus to keep His promise to forgive our sins and give us life forever. His forgiveness allows us to live in friendship with God, which ties right back into the big picture of the Bible.

As you read this book, questions will arise. *What is faith? What happens when you die? What will heaven be like?* When these questions come, refer to the read-aloud definitions in the glossary beginning on page 24. These will help you explain Bible concepts in a simple, clear way.

May God bless you as you lead your children in their journey toward faith.

—Charles F. Boyd

*John 1:12; 3:16–18, 36; 5:24; 6:47; 8:24; 11:25–26; 14:11; 20:31

For parents and teachers who have
no greater joy than to share
God's good news with children
in a way they can understand.

THE BIG PICTURE OF WHAT GOD HAS ALWAYS WANTED

CHARLES F. BOYD

Illustrations by
Heath McPherson

KIDS
Nashville, Tennessee

In the beginning, God created the heavens and the earth and everything in them. Sun, moon, stars . . . seas, land, mountains . . . grass, flowers, trees . . . fish, birds, animals . . . even creepy, crawly bugs. God liked the beautiful world He created very much.

God also created people. God created people so He could love them and they could love Him. God wanted His people to live in friendship with Him and with each other. He set things up so that living in friendship with God is the very best way to live. God placed the first man and the first woman in a wonderful garden and provided them with everything they needed. He told them to take care of the world He created. He told them to have families and fill up the whole planet with people who would love and enjoy Him forever. Everything was very good!

God desired that people find their highest happiness living with Him. But God did not make people to be robots who had to do what He said; He gave them a choice. They could live in friendship with God by trusting His goodness. Or they could live their own way and die trying.

Sadly, God's people did not trust Him. They selfishly disobeyed God and refused to do what He had said. They turned away from God, believing they could find happiness somewhere else.

As more and more families began to fill the earth, more and more people chose to live their own way rather than God's way. They lied to each other, hurt each other, fought with each other, and even killed each other. People thought they did not need God anymore. They refused to follow His ways. They even began to worship statues of wood and stone that they had made. People began to get sick and die. This was not the way things were supposed to be. It made God both sad and angry to see the people He loved hurting themselves and each other. Soon, the whole world—the good world that God created—was not so good anymore.

The people God loved needed to be rescued from their selfishness and all the hurt it caused.

So God put His plan in motion. God chose a man named Abraham and promised him that he would become the father of a great nation that God would bless. That nation was called Israel. God wanted the Israelites to be His special people so that, through them, He could make His love known to all peoples. Because Abraham believed God's promises, he was called the friend of God. Abraham didn't know it, but God planned that one of his great, great, great grandchildren would come to make things right between people and God again.

Commandments to teach them God's ways

Priests to remind them of God's love and forgiveness

God provided the people He loved with everything they needed to live in friendship with Him.

Kings to lead and guide them

Prophets to encourage and correct them

Because of God's blessing, Israel became a great nation just like God promised. But time after time, God's people turned away from Him to live selfish lives. Rather than acting like God's special people, they acted like people who didn't even know God. Even though the prophets urged the people to turn back to God, they still refused to love Him with all their hearts. Those same prophets began to tell of One who would come to make things right between people and God again.

You see, God would not give up on the people He loved. God knew that as long as people lived their lives for themselves, they would continue to die and be separated from His love forever.

So God sent His Son, Jesus, to tell His people He still loved them. One of Jesus' special names, *Immanuel*, means "God with us." Jesus came to show us what God is really like and what God has always wanted.

ABRAHAM was the father of Isaac, Jacob, Judah, Perez, Hezron, Ram, Amminadab, Nahshon, Salmon, Boaz, Obed, Jesse was the father of . . . David was the father of Solomon, Rehoboam, Abijah, Asa, Jehoshaphat, Joram Uzziah, Jotham, Ahaz, Hezekiah, Manasseh, Amon, Josiah, Jeconiah, Shealtiel, Zerubbabel, Abihud, Eliakim, Azor, Zadok, Achim, Eliud, Eleazar, Matthan, Jacob was the father of . . . Joseph, the husband of Mary by whom JESUS was born who is called the Messiah.
—MATTHEW 1:2–16

Jesus did many good things for people to show them God's love. He healed the sick. He fed people when they were hungry. He worked many amazing miracles. He even raised people from the dead.

Jesus loved *all* people—not just the best people. He even loved people who did bad things, which made some people angry. He liked to go to parties and tell stories of how God has always loved us and has always wanted us to come back home to Him.

And Jesus loved little children. He wanted them to be His friends, too.
He said, "Let the children come to Me; for the kingdom of heaven belongs
to everyone who comes to Me like them."

Jesus taught us how to live in friendship with God and each other. He said the most important commandment of all is to love God with all your heart. He also said to love other people like you love yourself. He knew that loving God and others is the very best way to live. Jesus also said He had the power to forgive people of their selfishness and wrongdoing. He promised that we could live with God now and forever if we would believe in Him.

Here's what He said, "Truly I tell you, everyone who believes in Me has eternal life." Many people did believe in Jesus and they became His friends and followers.

But others refused to believe in Him. They said, "We will not have this man tell us what to do." So they arrested Jesus. They told lies about Him. They beat Him and spat on Him. They killed Him by nailing Him to a big wooden cross. Everyone thought that was the end of Jesus.

But Jesus didn't stay dead. He came back to life and lots of people saw Him alive.

Before He went back to heaven, Jesus gathered His friends together. He explained how it had always been God's plan for Him to come to rescue people from their selfishness and death. He told them that He had to die for their sins and be raised from the dead in order to make things right between God and people again.

Then He commanded His friends to go into all the world and tell everyone the good news of God's love and forgiveness. He told them to invite everyone to come back into friendship with God by believing in Him. And because they did . . .

...Today, the church is a community made up of people from all over the world—people who want to follow Jesus and learn from Him how to live in friendship with God and others. Like Jesus, the church shows God's love by helping, serving, praying, and caring for others. Through the church, God continues to invite everyone to become a part of His family.

One day God will make everything new. He will make everything good again—just like it was in the beginning. In the kingdom of heaven there will be no more fighting or wars . . . no more sadness or sickness or death. And no more selfishness. The people who refused to live in friendship with God will not be in God's heaven. God has prepared a place for them where their selfishness cannot hurt anyone else ever again.

When God makes everything new, people from every nation will live with God and each other in peace forever. The whole world will be filled with people who know God and follow His ways. And God will love His people and His people will love Him . . .

Just like He always wanted.

What About You?

Did you know that God wants you to become one of His friends? To live in friendship with God is the best way to live. Do you remember what Jesus said you need to do to live with God now and forever? (*Believe in Him.*)

Trust

What do you think it means to believe in someone who makes you a promise? It means to trust her to do what she says she'll do. It's easy to believe in someone who made a promise to you and kept it. If a friend promises to come to your birthday party, you feel you can trust her if she has kept her other promises. If you didn't trust her, well, you probably wouldn't be very close friends, would you?

While we've all failed to keep our promises at some time or another, God *always* keeps His promises. Do you remember His promises?

• In the beginning, God created people to love Him and enjoy Him forever. But He told them that if they did not trust Him, they would die and be separated from Him.

• Later, God promised Abraham that his family would become a great nation. That nation, Israel, still exists today.

• And after Abraham died, God promised, through His prophets, that He would send someone who would rescue us from our selfishness and death.

About 2,000 years ago, God made good on all those promises by sending His Son, Jesus, to show us how to become God's friends again. Jesus promises that everyone who believes in Him will have eternal life. He promises to forgive our sins. So to believe in Jesus means to turn from our sin and selfishness and to trust Him to keep His promise to forgive our sins. It means to take Him at His Word.

Forgiveness

By dying on the cross, Jesus took the punishment we deserve, and He made forgiveness possible. Then by coming back to life, Jesus proved that He has the power to keep His promise to give us eternal life. Jesus has done everything that needs to be done for us to live in friendship with God forever.

Prayer

Do you want to become a friend of Jesus?
If you are ready, you can tell God you believe in Jesus right now.

Dear God, I want to be Your friend now and forever. Thank You for sending Jesus to forgive me of all my selfishness. Lord Jesus, I do believe in You. I believe You died for me and came back to life. I believe in Your promise to give me eternal life. I want You to know that I am turning from my selfishness and trusting You now as my Savior. Thank You for making it possible for me to live in friendship with God now and forever. Amen.

 The Bible to teach us

A Savior who shows us
God's love and forgiveness

God has provided us with everything
we need to live in friendship with Him.

 His very own Spirit living
inside us to guide us

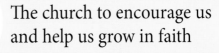 The church to encourage us
and help us grow in faith

Glossary

As you read and re-read this book to your children, questions will arise. The following definitions will help you explain biblical concepts in a way they can understand.

Bible

The Bible is God's story. It tells us what He is doing in this world and what He really wants. The Bible tells us how life really is—both the world we see and the world we can't see right now. It's also about people who can be both believing and unbelieving, good and bad at the same time, just like us.

Church

Sometimes we think of a church as a building. But when the Bible talks about the church, it's referring to people who are the friends and followers of Jesus. In other words, we don't really *go* to church, we *are* the church. Jesus wants His church to treat all people with love and respect—to treat them the way we want to be treated. If the church helps people in ways that show them God's love, then people who do not know God will see that God is real and that He wants all people to know Him.

Commandments

God gave His people commandments, or laws, to teach them how to live in friendship with God and each other. Simply obeying the commandments would not take people to heaven when they died. But obeying God's laws helped people live together happily with God and each other. Sadly, no one could ever keep all of God's commands perfectly. That's the specific way we "sin" against God—by not obeying His commandments. What's most important to understand is that when we don't do what God says, it's because we are not trusting that He is good and that His ways are best.

Death

God had planned for us to live with Him forever; but because people chose their own ways over God's, death came into the world. We will all die, yet Jesus promises that all of us who believe in Him will not stay dead forever after we die. God will bring us back to life with new, healthy bodies so we can live forever with Him.

Eternal Life

Eternal life with God is life that goes on forever and always, without stopping and without ever ending. It begins the moment we trust Jesus as our Savior, so it's not just something that happens to us after we die. It's having the best possible life now. Eternal life also means that once we have it, it cannot be taken away from us, and we can never lose it.

Faith, Belief, Trust

To "have faith" or to "trust in Jesus" means to believe He is who He says He is and He will do what He promised He would do. Jesus said that He, and He alone, was and is the way back to God. He promised to forgive sins and give eternal life to all who believe in Him. So to receive the life He offers, we must trust in Him and what He promises.

Forgiveness

When we forgive someone, it means we don't want to punish that person for hurting us. We can be friends with him or her again. When God forgives us, He no longer holds our sin against us. He promises to never bring it up again. When we ask His forgiveness, He forgives us completely. Not only are all our past sins forgiven, but so are all of the sins we will ever commit!

Friendship with God

There are several ways that the Bible describes living in a relationship with God. God is our Creator and we are His people. God is our King and we are His servants. God is our Shepherd and we are His sheep. God is our Father and we are His children. God is like a husband and we are like His wife. Friendship with God includes all these ideas. Most of all, friendship with God means coming to know Him so well that we trust what He says.

Jesus said to some people who were coming to trust Him more and more, "I no longer call you servants, but I call you friends." Jesus also said, "There is no greater love than for a person to lay down his life for his friends," and He laid down His life for us. He's a true friend. Living in friendship with Jesus is the very best way to live.

God

There is more about God that we don't know than we do know. What we do know about God comes from three places—creation, the Bible, and Jesus. The beauty of creation shows us that there must be a Creator who is powerful and wise and like no other. The Bible reveals to us that behind the scenes of history there is a God who is with us and for us. Jesus shows us what God is like in person—loving, caring, powerful, pure, and true.

In the Bible, God reveals Himself to us in three persons—Father, Son, and Holy Spirit. We call this the "Trinity." It's hard to understand how God is three in one and one in three. But it's kind of like how water can be a liquid, a gas (steam), and a solid (ice). Or, how we say that an egg has a yolk (the yellow part), a white, and a shell. Three in one, one in three. While no illustrations like these can perfectly describe our great God, remember this: God knows us and loves us, and wants us to live in friendship with Him now and forever. And, Jesus, who is God in a human body, came to make that possible.

God's Plan

We learn later on in the Bible that from before time began God knew what He was going to do. For whatever reason, God chose to make people enough like Himself so they could enjoy living in friendship with Him. But He did not force them to do what He said. Sadly, they chose to turn away from God. Then sin and death spread to everyone. This made God both sad and angry, but it did not catch Him by surprise. He knew that, when all was said and done, He Himself would have to come and do for us what we could not do for ourselves—that is, give us new hearts that could love and trust Him forever. That way, we would really see how good God is and how much He loves us. Jesus' death on the cross shows us how far God is willing to go to give us new hearts.

Heaven

Heaven is the place where Jesus is. Before he died, Jesus said he was going back to heaven to prepare a place for His followers to join Him after they died. In one of Jesus' favorite stories, the kingdom of heaven is described as a great big party where everyone is invited. In heaven, people will celebrate God and His love forever. All the things we love about this world will be much better in heaven.

Hell

Hell is the place where people who refuse to live in friendship with God go after they die. If we don't want to live in friendship with God now, God will not force us to live with Him after we die. According to the Bible, people in hell are tormented forever by the fact that nothing they do from that point on can bring them to God.

Holy Spirit

After we believe in Jesus, God puts His very own Spirit inside us. The Holy Spirit guides us to live in ways that reflect God's love to others. He helps us remember what God says and He lets us know when we act selfishly. Then He nudges us to admit we are wrong and to accept God's forgiveness to start new.

Jesus

Jesus is our Savior—the One promised by the prophets who would come to rescue us from our sin. It took only a short time for people to realize that Jesus wasn't like anybody they had ever met. He healed the sick, raised the dead, cast out demons, and fed thousands of people with a little boy's sack lunch. Even the winds and the waves obeyed His command. When Jesus taught about God, people were astonished by what He said and how He said it because they were getting to know God in a fresh, new way.

The story of Jesus is recorded in the Bible books of Matthew, Mark, Luke, and John. As you read the stories of Jesus, you will see that no one ever lived the way Jesus lived. No one ever spoke the way He spoke. No one ever loved the way He loved. Jesus shows us what God is really like. He shows us what God wants us to be like. He came to teach us how to live in friendship with God and people again.

Satan (the Devil)

From the beginning of our time, God's desire to live in friendship with the people He loves has been opposed by Satan (the "serpent of old," who is called the Devil). Satan is God's enemy, but not God's evil equal. In no way is he as powerful as God, but Satan and his evil angels (demons) try to make people believe that God is not good and God's ways are not fair. But one day, God will be done with him. God will cast the Devil into hell so he will not be able to bother God's people ever again.

Sin

Sin is choosing to live the way we want rather than how God wants. It's the selfish "I want my way" kind of attitude that is in all of us. The desire to live our way rather than God's way separates us from Him and the life He wants for us. It keeps us from loving God and others the way God wants. This is why there is so much hurt and fighting in the world today—some of us have chosen to live our lives to make ourselves happy without caring about what God thinks.

How This Book Came to Be

The vision for a book that would set forth the big idea of the Bible came to me years ago. A man with no church background asked me, "What's the Bible about anyway?" As I attempted to answer, I found it was much more difficult than I expected. He didn't understand the Christianese I had become so comfortable speaking. So he continued asking questions—"In the beginning, what did God want? What went wrong? Why is the world the way it is today? What is God doing to make things right again? How will it all end?" Those questions helped me break things down into a simple explanation of our faith.

I've had further opportunities to share the gospel from a storyline approach rather than a fact-based presentation. When presented as a story, the message seems to resonate with people having little or no Bible knowledge. After hearing the gospel set in the larger story of Scripture, one businessman put it this way, "I'm not sure I'm ready to buy in, but for the first time in my life, I understand it."

A while back, as I listened to children's baptismal testimonies, I realized that most kids are influenced to follow Christ through the encouragement of parents and teachers. No big "aha" there, but then the thought hit me, *We're not equipping parents to share the gospel with their children in a way they can understand.* Just like the businessman who needed someone to explain the gospel free of Christian jargon, children need the same thing. They need to hear God's Story told in a simple, biblically-accurate way. For that reason, I wrote *The Big Picture of What God Has Always Wanted* to help parents pass their faith on to their children.

Acknowledgments

Many people have contributed valuable ideas and input that have shaped the final outcome of *The Big Picture of What God Has Always Wanted*: Karen Boyd, Beth Beutler, Kerry Buttram, Paul and Lisa Clark, Jo Dillard, Laurie Glass, Cindy Griner, Mike Hawkins, Lori Johnson, David and Elaine Martin, Mark Moody, Betty Moran, Craig and Karen O'Neal, Brian Onken, Art and Suzanne Ringger, Minda Shelton, Laura Smith, Raydell Tedder, Bob Wilkin, Steven Mathewson, Steve Farrar, John Walton, and Haddon Robinson.

Gregg Stutts, the former director of publishing at FamilyLife®, became a champion for the book and made it happen. Thanks, Gregg.

Also, with my book now being published by Lifeway, I would like to thank Dr. George Guthrie for bringing the book to the attention of Dan Lynch and his team at B&H Kids. Thanks, George and Dan, and thank you, Trevin Wax, for making *The Big Picture of What God Has Always Wanted* a part of The Gospel Project.

Heath McPherson, thanks for bringing the story to life and capturing the imaginations of children and adults through your masterful illustrations.

© 2013 by B&H Publishing Group
Nashville, Tennessee
Text © 2013 by Charles F. Boyd

Produced in cooperation with FamilyLife® Publishing
Little Rock, Arkansas

Scripture taken from the NEW AMERICAN STANDARD
BIBLE®, Copyright © 1960, 1963, 1968, 1971, 1972, 1973, 1975,
1977, 1995 by The Lockman Foundation. Used by permission.

The quotations attributed to Jesus on pages 15 and 16
are paraphrases of actual quotations from Scripture
(Matthew 19:14 and John 6:47, respectively).

ISBN: 978-1-4336-8022-9

Dewey Decimal Classification: C231.7
Subject Heading: GOD \ BIBLE STORIES \ GOSPEL

1 2 3 4 5 6 7 8 • 17 16 15 14 13